an easy-read ACTIVITY book

COIN FUN

by Ken Reisberg

illustrations by Nina Gaelen

DISCARD

Franklin Watts
New York/London/Toronto/Sydney
1981

To Doris,
for giving me what money couldn't buy

R.L. 3.0 Spache Revised Formula

Library of Congress Cataloging in Publication Data

Reisberg, Ken.
    Coin fun.

    (An easy-read activity book)
    Summary: Briefly discusses coins and suggests
coin tricks, games, and puzzles.
    1. Coin tricks—Juvenile literature.   2. Coins
—Juvenile literature.   [1. Coin tricks.
2. Coins.   3. Magic tricks] I. Gaelen, Nina.
II. Title.   III. Series: Easy-read activity book.
GV1559.R44   793.8   81-122
ISBN 0-531-04307-X   AACR2

CONTENTS

WHAT ARE COINS?

Before money came into use, people used handy objects when they bought things they wanted. Sometimes they used shells or stones. And sometimes they used beads. But this was not an easy way to pay for things. So people made little round disks. Each disk, or **coin**, told what its **value**, or worth, was. Later, paper money was made. Coins may cost more to make than paper money, but they last for a longer time.

Coins have always been popular. They are easy to handle and easy to carry. Coins don't tear. For these reasons, coins are used by people all over the world.

Coins come in all sizes, colors, and shapes. Once they were made from rare metals like silver and gold. But now they are made from nickel, zinc, and copper.

4

DO YOU KNOW OUR COINS?

The most common coins in the United States are:

penny 1 cent, or 1/100th of a dollar

  **nickel** 5 cents, or 1/20th of a dollar

dime 10 cents, or 1/10th of a dollar

  **quarter** 25 cents, or 1/4 of a dollar

half dollar 50 cents, or 1/2 of a dollar

Each coin is a different size and is made of different kinds of material. But all these coins are the same in these ways:

- they are round
- they all have pictures of past Presidents on the front, or **obverse**, side
- they all have the words "IN GOD WE TRUST" on the front
- the worth, or value, of the coin is shown on the back, or **reverse**, side

- they all have the words "E PLURIBUS UNUM" on the back. These Latin words are made up of 13 letters. That is the same as the number of the 13 colonies that formed our nation. The words mean "One out of many."

Coin games, coin tricks, and coin puzzles are only a pocket's reach away. You can play with one or more people. You can play with pennies, nickels, dimes, and quarters. Save your coins in order to play. You will find that coin fun is one of the best kinds of fun you can have.

THE QUARTERBACK COIN TRICK

Tell your friends that you have an extra quarter. If they want to get it, all they have to do is pick it up off the floor!

1. Place the quarter on the floor about a foot or two from the wall. Then ask one of your friends to stand against the wall so that her heels are touching it.

2. Tell this friend to pick up the quarter. She cannot move her heels or bend her knees. Your friends can try to pick up the quarter as often as they want to. No matter how hard they try, they will fail and you will get your quarter back.

The Secret

Your friends will not be able to pick up the coin without losing their balance and falling forward.

DID YOU KNOW THAT
the bald eagle on the back of the quarter is our national bird? Many people had wanted the turkey to be picked as our national bird, but the eagle was chosen for its strength and beauty.

THE TRAVELING QUARTER GAME

Number of players: 2
You will need: a quarter

How to Play

Sit on one side of a table. Ask a friend to sit facing you on the other side. Hit the quarter with one finger from your side to the other side of the table. If the coin falls short of the target, hit it again. Stop when the quarter falls over the table or balances on the edge. Your friend then takes his or her turn at play. Score one point each time the coin is hit to the edge of the table. The first player to score five points wins the game.

DID YOU KNOW THAT
the place where coins are made is called a mint? The word **mint** comes from a Latin word that was part of the name for the goddess of money.

THE SHAKE AND BAKE COIN TRICK

1. Place five pennies on a table.

2. Tell your friend he or she is to pick up one of the coins. The friend should make a tight fist and then shake the coin in the fist for ten seconds while your back is turned. Then the coin should be put back on the table.

3. Now face your friend. Tell him or her that the coin from the fist is still shaking! To prove it, you will pick it out from the others.

4. Touch each coin and then hold up the secret coin for everyone to see.

The Secret Copper holds heat. The tightly held coin will feel warmer than the others.

DID YOU KNOW THAT
there were $10 and $20 gold coins issued in
the United States in 1907?

4 THE PALMS AWAY TRICK

1. Extend one hand out, with the palm facing upward. Place a dime in the center of that same palm.

2. Ask your friend to take a hairbrush and see if she can remove the dime from your hand.

3. Tell her to brush the dime as hard as she likes, but that she must hold the brush level at all times.

DID YOU KNOW THAT
the first metal coins were made in ancient
China? Many coins made over 2,000 years
ago, in Greece and in Rome, still exist.

4 **The Secret**: The soft bristles on the brush move in opposite directions. While the dime is being pushed forward, it is also being pulled backward.

5 THE HIT-THE-PENNY GAME

Number of players: 2
You will need: a ball, chalk, a penny

Put a penny on the ground. Draw two chalk lines about 5 feet (1.5 m) on either side of the coin. Stand behind one line. Ask your friend to stand facing you behind the other line. Take turns throwing the ball. Aim for the penny. Each time you hit the penny, count 1 point. If you hit the penny and it flips over, count 2 points. The penny should stay wherever the ball hits it. The first player who makes 11 points wins the game.

DID YOU KNOW THAT
there were ½-cent coins issued in the United States between 1792 and 1857? And there were 2-cent coins in circulation from 1864 until 1873.

THE COINS AND CAP TRICK

1. Find three bottle caps or jar covers that are exactly the same and put them on a table in a straight line. Place a dime under the one in the middle.

2. Tell your friend that you will prove to him that the hand is quicker than the eye. Move the caps around quickly, changing their positions for several seconds. Now ask your friend to point to the cap that covers the coin.

3. Lift the cap to see if he has guessed correctly.

DID YOU KNOW THAT
the Jefferson nickel, first issued in 1938,
was chosen as the result of a
competition?

The Secret
The hand truly can be quicker than the eye. The
faster you move the bottle caps, the harder it will
be for your friend to tell which cap holds the coin.

7 THE TRICKY TRIANGLE PUZZLE

1. Make a triangle with ten pennies.

2. Ask your friends to try to form a new triangle that points down. Tell them they can only move three pennies.

20

The Secret

Move penny #7 to penny #2. Move penny #10 next to penny #3. Place penny #1 below pennies #8 and #9 and between them. When you do this, the triangle will point downward.

DID YOU KNOW THAT
early pennies were very large and could be used by frontier people as rifle sights?

THE KICK-THE-COIN GAME

Number of players: 2 to 8
You will need: chalk, 2 nickels

How to Play

Mark a starting or GO line with chalk. Make another line about 10 feet (3 m) away. Place two nickels behind the GO line. Stand behind one nickel. Ask your friend to stand behind the other one. Kick your coin past the far line and back again. The first player who crosses back across the GO line wins.

DID YOU KNOW THAT
coin collectors handle coins only by their
edges so that the surfaces do not
get worn?

23

THE TOUCH AND GO COIN TRICK

1. Place a dime, a penny, and a nickel on the table as shown.

2. Ask a friend to put the nickel in between the touching penny and dime. Tell her that she must do it without *moving* the penny and without *touching* the dime.

DID YOU KNOW THAT
Alaska was purchased for over seven million dollars and that there are coin collections worth more than this amount?

The Secret

Place the middle fingertip of your left hand firmly on the penny. Put the middle fingertip of your right hand on the nickel. Now strike the penny with the nickel by sliding the nickel into it. If you strike the penny strongly, the dime will move. You can now simply pick up the nickel and place it between the penny and dime.

THE CHANGE-A-SHAPE PUZZLE

1. Make a square by placing seven pennies and five nickels as shown.

2. Ask a friend to try and make the square into another shape with five coins on each side.

Clue: the new shape has three sides!

26

DID YOU KNOW THAT
many people like to collect coins? The study
of coins, tokens, and paper money is called
numismatics (new-miz-MAT-icks). People
collect coins because they like to and also
because old coins can be very valuable.

The Secret Don't move the pennies at all. Move the nickels to form a triangle.

THE COIN CATCHER GAME

Number of players: 1 or more
You will need: pennies

How to Play

Stand with your right arm extended out on a line with your shoulder. Your palm should face upward. Put a coin on the crease of that same arm. Now relax your muscles and let your arm drop quickly to your side. As the coin falls, try to catch it with your right hand.

You can play this game with your friends. Use one, two, or more coins to see who is the champion coin catcher.

DID YOU KNOW THAT

old coins tell us about the past? The faces and pictures on coins tell us about the people who used them and how they lived. You would be surprised to find out what you can learn from the coins in your very own pockets!

THE COIN TWISTER TRICK

1. Secretly put a dime and a nickel inside your hand. Then make a fist.

2. Say to your friends: "I am holding two coins which add up to fifteen cents, but one of them isn't a dime."

3. Ask your friends what coins you are holding. You will be very surprised at the answers you will get.

The Secret One of the coins isn't a dime, since one of them is a nickel.

THE IMPOSSIBLE COIN TRICK

1. Draw a straight line on a piece of paper.
2. Show three nickels. Ask a friend to place them so that you can see the "heads" side of two nickels on one side of the line and the "tails" side of two nickels on the other.

The Secret

Stand one nickel up on edge on the line between
the other two. Practice letting your hand go and
seeing if you can balance the coin without
touching it. If you can do this well, your audience
will like it.

14 STARING AT A COIN

1. Tell a friend that when you stare at a coin it makes a reflection in your eyes. To prove this, give your friend a penny to hold in one hand and a dime for the other.

2. Walk out of sight into a nearby room.

3. Tell your friend to raise either coin to eye level. Then the friend should stare closely at the coin for a full minute. Then he should put it back to his side.

4. After your friend has done this, return to the room. Look into your friend's eyes. Then tell him which coin was the one he stared at.

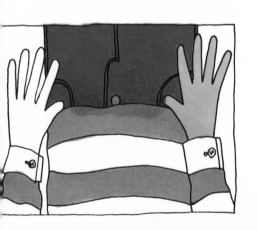

 The Secret
Only pretend to look for the reflection of the coin in your friend's eyes. Instead, look at his hands. The hand which held the coin will be lighter and more pale than the other.

DID YOU KNOW THAT
"IN GOD WE TRUST" must appear on all United States coins, as the result of an Act passed by Congress in 1955?